Love is Everywhere

Copyright © 2025 by Tiffany Celeste Frenette

All rights reserved.

No part of this book may be reproduced, shared, or used in any form or by any means, including photocopying or recording, without written permission from the publisher, except for brief quotations used for review or educational purposes with proper credit.

Pebble Byway Press
Toronto, Canada

Written by: Tiffany Celeste Frenette
Edited by: Christine Marrin
Illustrated by: Georgia Lesley

Layout and design by Corey Szames and Tiffany Celeste Frenette
Special thanks to Asha Frost, Iffath Lotallah and Carlyle Mark

For more information or to contact the author, visit
celestefrenette.com

To see more of the author's work:

Visit IG: @celestefrenette
FB @celestefrenette
TikTok @celestefrenette

ISBN (Trade Paperback): 978-1-7778634-7-0

ISBN (E-book): 978-1-7778634-8-7

First edition
December 2025

Printed with care and love for young readers.

Love is Everywhere

Written By: Tiffany Celeste Frenette

Illustrated By: Georgia Lesley

For my children, Jaiden and Mirahbelle.

When I look into your eyes,
I see God.
When I hear your laughter,
I hear God.
When I think of how much I love you,
I feel God.

And for all who sometimes forget,
may you remember the source energy you are made of.
May you remember that God is love,
and may you find that love
everywhere.

Jaiden was such a curious boy. He wondered about little things, like what a bearded dragon eats, what makes a rainbow, and what happens when you melt marshmallows and stir in chocolate chips.

One morning, he woke up with a question that felt big and important. He hurried to find his mom so he could ask her.

"Mama," he said, "where is God?"
His mother smiled.
"God is everywhere, Jaiden."

Everywhere? Jaiden felt excited. If God was everywhere, it shouldn't be hard to find him.

Determined, he ran up to his room. "Are you here, God?" he asked.

He waited, but nothing happened. So the search began.

Jaiden zipped downstairs and headed for the door when his mom called out, "Sweetie, don't forget your jacket."

Jaiden often forgot things like that when he was excited.
His mom didn't want him to be cold, so she always reminded him.
With a big smile he told her, "I'm going to go look for God!"

Outside, it was a beautiful sunny day. Jaiden walked slowly, looking closely at everything around him. He didn't know what God looked like, so he searched with curiosity and wonder. "Where are you, God?" he asked.

Suddenly, he heard a sound. Peeking from behind a tree, he saw a family of deer. He gasped with delight.
"Could this be God?" he wondered.
The biggest deer looked at him calmly, then went back to eating. Jaiden smiled and continued on his way.

Soon the sky turned gray and rain began to fall. Jaiden saw his neighbour nearby.
"Oh Jaiden," he said kindly, "it's starting to rain. I'll walk you home."
"I can't," Jaiden said. "I have to find God."
He ran off so fast that he splashed right through a big puddle.

At last, Jaiden reached a place where he was sure he would find God. "I bet God is here," he thought, gazing up at the tall church doors.

He ran inside and was so happy because standing right there in front of him was God! At least he was pretty sure it was God!

"Are you God?" he asked a woman standing nearby.

She laughed softly and patted him on the head.
"Oh no, dear," she said. "I'm just the cleaning lady."

Jaiden stepped back outside, feeling confused. He sighed and looked up at the sky. "Mama said you are everywhere," he sighed, "but I can't find you anywhere."

Cold, wet, and tired, Jaiden arrived home. His mom was there waiting. She helped him take off his wet clothes. "What's wrong, sweetheart?" she asked.

"I looked all day," Jaiden said. "But God wasn't anywhere."

His mom sat beside him. "Oh love," she said gently, "you can't see God." Jaiden frowned. "But you said God is everywhere."

Jaiden curled up beside his mom and rested his head on her lap. She stroked his hair and smiled. "God *is* everywhere," she said. "God isn't a he or a she. God isn't a person you can point to. God is the love in our hearts, and love is everywhere."

That night, Jaiden stood by his window and looked at the moon and stars. He thought about what his mom had said.

As he slept, Jaiden dreamed.
In his dream, a calm and steady voice called his name.
"Jaiden."

He found himself standing in a quiet field under the moonlight.
"God?" he asked.
"Yes," the voice replied. "It's me."

"Where were you?" Jaiden asked. "I looked for you all day."

"Oh Jaiden," God said, "you saw me many times."
Jaiden's eyes widened. "I did?"

"Yes," God replied. "I was everywhere, because I am everything."
"I am the strong oak tree. I am the peaceful deer. I am the rain. I am your neighbour who offered help. I am the cleaning lady. I am the loving touch of your mother. I am everything. I am love."

Now Jaiden understood.
He drifted back into sleep and rested deeply until morning.
He awoke feeling happy and peaceful.

Sunlight filled the kitchen as Jaiden sat at the table with his mom. "Did you sleep well, sweetie?" she asked. "Yes," he said. "I understand now."

"God is the sun and the trees and the animals and our neighbors," Jaiden said.
"And love."
"Yes, love," his mom replied.

Jaiden paused. "Is God even me, Mama?"

She smiled. "Yes. Especially you."
"And you too?" he asked. "Yes," she said.

Jaiden thought for a moment, then smiled. "God must be really beautiful." His mom looked at him with love. "The most beautiful of all."

About the Author

Celeste is a mama who loves her children, nature, and asking big questions. She likes quiet moments, kind people, and noticing love in everyday life. She wrote this book to share something she believes with children everywhere: love is everywhere, and you are love too.

After the Story

You just finished Jaiden's story.
Let's wonder together.

What was your favourite part of the story?

Where did Jaiden look for God?

Where do you see love?

Who makes you feel loved?

How do you feel when someone is kind to you?

How can you show love today?

Take a quiet moment to remember:
You are love.
     Love is everywhere.

Where do you see love?
draw it here

Caregiver Prompts

This story invites big questions and quiet feelings. Children may respond with curiosity, insight, confusion, or silence. All of these are welcome. You do not need to explain or correct. Listening is enough.

If your child shares an idea, try reflecting it back:
"That's interesting."
"I hadn't thought of it that way."
"Tell me more."

If your child asks what God is, you might say:
"What do you think God is?"

If your child says they see God or love somewhere unexpected, allow it.
There is no right or wrong place to notice love.

If your child feels unsure or confused, you can reassure them:
"It's okay not to know."
"Big questions don't need quick answers."

You may invite expression beyond words.
Drawing, quiet time, or play can help children process what they feel.
Remember that children learn most from how we are with them.
Your presence, kindness, and curiosity
teach more than explanations ever could.

This book is not meant to define beliefs, but to open hearts.

Wonder together.
Let love lead.

Author's Note

I grew up in a Christian environment, learning about God through church, school, and the Bible. As I got older, my relationship with God continued to unfold, and my understanding began to widen. I started to notice God not only in places of worship, but in nature, in quiet moments, in the kindness of strangers, and in the eyes of my children.

I stopped waiting for prayer to speak to God and realized I could speak anytime. God no longer felt like something outside of me, but something I experienced as love itself.

Later, through my work as a nurse in palliative care, this understanding deepened. Sitting with people at the end of their lives, I witnessed something profound. As everything else fell away, love remained. It was what people offered, what they wanted to give, and what they hoped to leave behind. In those moments, it became clear to me that love is who we are at our core.

I also found myself reflecting on the story of creation. If, in the beginning, there was only God, then everything that came into being must have come from that same source. To me, this meant that love is not separate from us, but expressed through us, through people, through nature, and through everyday acts of kindness.

Love Is Everywhere was written as an invitation to wonder. To gently open space for curiosity, compassion, and connection.

If this story helps children grow up feeling connected to their source, and seeing themselves and others as worthy, sacred, and deeply loved, then it has done what it came here to do.

www.ingramcontent.com/pod-product-compliance
Lightning Source LLC
Chambersburg PA
CBHW061400090426
42743CB00002B/91